113th Congress
2d Session

Printed for the use of the
Commission on Security and Cooperation in Europe

THE DOG BARKS, BUT THE CARAVAN MOVES ON: HIGHS AND LOWS IN U.S.-RUSSIAN RELATIONS

MARCH 27, 2014

**Briefing of the
Commission on Security and Cooperation in Europe**

Washington: 2015

Commission on Security and Cooperation in Europe
234 Ford House Office Building
Washington, DC 20515
202–225–1901
csce@mail.house.gov
http://www.csce.gov

Legislative Branch Commissioners

SENATE

BENJAMIN L. CARDIN, MARYLAND,
    Chairman
SHELDON WHITEHOUSE, RHODE ISLAND
TOM UDALL, NEW MEXICO
JEANNE SHAHEEN, NEW HAMPSHIRE
RICHARD BLUMENTHAL, CONNECTICUT
ROGER WICKER, MISSISSIPPI
SAXBY CHAMBLISS, GEORGIA
JOHN BOOZMAN, ARKANSAS

HOUSE

CHRISTOPHER SMITH, NEW JERSEY,
    Co-Chairman
JOSEPH PITTS, PENNSYLVANIA
ROBERT ADERHOLT, ALABAMA
PHIL GINGREY, GEORGIA
MICHAEL BURGESS, TEXAS
ALCEE HASTINGS, FLORIDA
LOUISE McINTOSH SLAUGHTER,
    NEW YORK
MIKE McINTYRE, NORTH CAROLINA
STEVE COHEN, TENNESSEE

(II)

ABOUT THE ORGANIZATION FOR SECURITY AND COOPERATION IN EUROPE

The Helsinki process, formally titled the Conference on Security and Cooperation in Europe, traces its origin to the signing of the Helsinki Final Act in Finland on August 1, 1975, by the leaders of 33 European countries, the United States and Canada. As of January 1, 1995, the Helsinki process was renamed the Organization for Security and Cooperation in Europe (OSCE). The membership of the OSCE has expanded to 56 participating States, reflecting the breakup of the Soviet Union, Czechoslovakia, and Yugoslavia.

The OSCE Secretariat is in Vienna, Austria, where weekly meetings of the participating States' permanent representatives are held. In addition, specialized seminars and meetings are convened in various locations. Periodic consultations are held among Senior Officials, Ministers and Heads of State or Government.

Although the OSCE continues to engage in standard setting in the fields of military security, economic and environmental cooperation, and human rights and humanitarian concerns, the Organization is primarily focused on initiatives designed to prevent, manage and resolve conflict within and among the participating States. The Organization deploys numerous missions and field activities located in Southeastern and Eastern Europe, the Caucasus, and Central Asia. The website of the OSCE is: <www.osce.org>.

ABOUT THE COMMISSION ON SECURITY AND COOPERATION IN EUROPE

The Commission on Security and Cooperation in Europe, also known as the Helsinki Commission, is a U.S. Government agency created in 1976 to monitor and encourage compliance by the participating States with their OSCE commitments, with a particular emphasis on human rights.

The Commission consists of nine members from the United States Senate, nine members from the House of Representatives, and one member each from the Departments of State, Defense and Commerce. The positions of Chair and Co-Chair rotate between the Senate and House every two years, when a new Congress convenes. A professional staff assists the Commissioners in their work.

In fulfilling its mandate, the Commission gathers and disseminates relevant information to the U.S. Congress and the public by convening hearings, issuing reports that reflect the views of Members of the Commission and/or its staff, and providing details about the activities of the Helsinki process and developments in OSCE participating States.

The Commission also contributes to the formulation and execution of U.S. policy regarding the OSCE, including through Member and staff participation on U.S. Delegations to OSCE meetings. Members of the Commission have regular contact with parliamentarians, government officials, representatives of non-governmental organizations, and private individuals from participating States. The website of the Commission is: <www.csce.gov>.

THE DOG BARKS, BUT THE CARAVAN MOVES ON: HIGHS AND LOWS IN U.S.-RUSSIAN RELATIONS

MARCH 27, 2014

COMMISSIONER

(IV)

THE DOG BARKS, BUT THE CARAVAN MOVES ON: HIGHS AND LOWS IN U.S.-RUSSIAN RELATIONS

March 27, 2014

Commission on Security and Cooperation in Europe
Washington, DC

The briefing was held from 1:03 to 2:41 p.m. EST in 2103 Rayburn House Office Building, Washington, D.C., Kyle Parker, Policy Adviser, CSCE, presiding.

Mr. PARKER. Ladies and gentlemen, it's just after 1:00. My name's Kyle Parker. I'm on the policy staff here at the Commission on Security and Cooperation in Europe. I cover Russia. It's my pleasure to welcome you all on behalf of Senator Ben Cardin, chairman of the commission; Congressman Chris Smith, our co-chairman; and all of our commissioners. I welcome you to today's briefing, The Dog Barks, but the Caravan Moves On: Highs and Lows in U.S.-Russia relations."

Russia-watchers in the audience will be familiar with this saying, but for those just tuning in, it's a proverb from the east that Russian President Vladimir Putin, among others, is fond of quoting. Vladimir Putin, as many of you know, is highly quotable.

A new and fearsome era has dawned, and we at the commission felt it appropriate to mark the moment and begin a discussion examining where we've been in hopes that the past might offer insight into where we could be headed in our bilateral relations with the Russian Federation. Interest in Russia on Capitol Hill is at a post-Cold War high, but the knowledge base lags far behind what it once was and should be strengthened for a properly informed foreign policy.

Today we hope to make a small contribution toward remedying this with a lively and on-the-record discussion that will be the start of many public conversations about whether and how we should attempt to reconcile what appear to be irreconcilable differences between Moscow and Washington.

We begin with the assumption that the current state of the relationship is undesirable and that U.S.-Russian cooperation across a range of vital interests should continue. I was just skimming headlines on the way over and came across a punchy one from National Journal: "At Least Russia and the U.S. Still Get Along in Outer Space." Nothing should be taken for granted given current atmospherics, but we should be able to do a lot better than that. But how, and at what cost?

By the way, anyone here should feel free to challenge this assumption or anything else during our discussion period. We have world-class experts on the panel and in the audience and the flexibility for a genuine conversation. I encourage all to keep that in mind during the presentations and feel free to be direct and provocative in any response or question.

We posed a number of questions in the briefing notice, and I hope that by the end of today's event, we'll have offered at least the beginning of something approaching an answer.

Helping us with this daunting task is the University of Maine's Jim Warhola and we are waiting but will hopefully show soon the Kennan Institute's Matt Rojansky. Their bios are on the table outside.

Matt directs the Wilson Center's Kennan Institute, which is certainly the premier center for Soviet and post-Soviet studies here in Washington and among the leading institutes in the field worldwide. I tip the Commission's hat to the Kennan Institute as something of an older brother from the détente era. Kennan was founded in 1974, and our humble commission in 1976. In between these years, in 1975, the Helsinki Final Act was signed, a document we've heard referenced on multiple occasions around the ongoing crisis in Ukraine.

Jim Warhola came all the way from Orono, Maine, to be with us today. Thank you, Jim, for braving yesterday's nor'easter, and we appreciate the University of Maine sending you on TDY to Washington so we can all benefit from your fascinating research into a vital relationship at the center of comprehensive security and cooperation in Europe, which is quite literally almost our middle name.

We'll start with Jim's presentation and then turn to Matt for a wrap of what we heard from Jim and guidance on the perennial question of what is to be done. Following Matt's remarks, we'll open the floor to hear from all of you.

Before I turn it over to Jim, I want to recognize Congressman Aderholt, our commissioner for any remarks he'd like to offer. Congressman?

Mr. ADERHOLT. Thank you for being here. We just got out of votes. I wanted to come by and so look forward to hearing the testimony here.

Mr. PARKER. Well, sir, we're honored to have you.

Jim, your show.

Mr. WARHOLA. Thank you very much. Thank you very much, Kyle, and the commission for your invitation to come here and to share some of my thoughts about the current state of U.S.-Russian relations and where we might go from here. I'm very honored to be here. And thank you all for coming. Thank you for—once again for the invitation for our Russian friends and our Russian guests

Mr. PARKER. Jim, could you speak a little bit louder?

Mr. WARHOLA. Of course.

I just greeted our Russian guests. No one in this room needs to be informed that the state of U.S.-Russian relations right now is not good. The question is where do we go from here. There is no easy or simple answer to that question. Nobody wants war. They don't want it in the hinterlands of the United States. I'm equally confident they don't want it in Russia or anywhere else.

The question of how should the United States relate to Russia, I think, is on the minds of everyone here in the United States and also, the preoccupation of those in Russia itself.

There are a range of views I think that one could take to understand this. On the one hand, we might view Russia as an implacable, mortal threat. On the other hand, view Russia as the best of friends. We're clearly not that right now. The truth is, it's probably somewhere in between. Could we be a value-based cooperator, an interest-based cooperator, a neutral partner, perhaps some sort of wary tolerance? And again, there is no easy answer to this—how should the United States of America relate to Russia?

To begin answering that question, I'm reminded of a little Russian proverb. And it's pretty old, and even some of my Russian friends didn't quite recall it, but I've been told from long ago that—and the Russian proverb says that if you neglect history, you lose one eye. If you forget history, you lose two eyes. It seems to me that the last thing that the United States of America needs right now, the last thing that the Russian Federation needs right now, is to forget history.

What I'd like to do today is just spend a few minutes talking about some of my research on the long-term patterns, or what the French call the longue durée, of U.S.-Russian relations. U.S.-Russian relations were established formally, diplomatically in 1809, and they continue to this day. There was an interruption, of course, after the Russian Revolution in 1917 until they were re-established in 1934. But except that period, they have continued uninterrupted.

The project—I won't read the whole 180-page manuscript that I've written on this theme, but I will read you a few excerpts from it. Here's what I did.

Mr. PARKER. Not to interrupt, but Jim, we do have it here in one chart, hopefully some of you have availed yourselves of the handouts.

Mr. WARHOLA. Also, the list of references, if you could circulate that too.

Mr. PARKER. Yeah. Please.

Mr. WARHOLA. Here's what I decided to do, and I started this several years ago, is I looked at all of the references to either Russia, Soviet Union, Kremlin, anything related to Russia in all of the presidential State of the Union addresses given by every American president ever since the first State of the Union address was given by George Washington in 1790. And I asked Kyle to print up a list of all those references that are in the process of being circulated now.

To see if we could see any patterns—again, remembering that old Russian proverb, as you may know: If you neglect history, you lose one eye. If you forget history, you lose two eyes. So it seemed to me appropriate to look into the long-term patterns of U.S.-Russian relations. How have U.S. and Russia related to each other, once again, over what the French call the longue durée?

Here, if you'll indulge me, I will read a few paragraphs and only a few paragraphs from the manuscript that I've got. But even before doing it, it seems to me that—it's important to remember—these are grave matters. We're talking about not only life and death matters but also the fate of the United States and the fate of the Russian Federation and a lot of other people too. It's useful perhaps to remember that, back to the days of the ancient—in the classical world, there were four recognized cardinal virtues: wisdom, justice, courage and moderation.

One of those virtues, it seems—or two—they're all, of course, essential in these circumstances, particularly in these highly tense circumstances, but particularly the two virtues of courage and of moderation. Courage to be able to perhaps see things from another's point of view is a foundational starting point for possibly building bridges, for establishing some sort of reconciliation, for perhaps beginning to understand: what does Moscow see when it looks at the world? What does Washington see when it looks at the world? That takes a certain amount of courage on our part, intellectual courage and moral courage, if we dare say so.

The other cardinal virtue—again, there were four: wisdom, justice, courage, moderation—of moderation, was explicated by Aristotle in his great work Politics, and I'll not go into that here, but Aristotle's point is that in most circumstances, these other virtues, wisdom and justice, are to be found between the middle point between two opposing vices. It seems to me that in our disposition to Russia—even before we begin to get into some of the details of this—that in our disposition to Russia, that moderation is called for, to tone down as—and again, I'm not unaware of the fact that military capability is being ratcheted up even as we speak—on both sides. Moderation it seems to me is absolutely critical, moderation in the form so avoiding on the one hand perhaps what—a view that I would consider to be extreme, that is, that we need to get "tough on Russia", and we need to—"damn it!—we need to, just load up the guns, and if—and if they move, we're going to start blasting." I don't find that productive. I don't think it's useful, not in the short run, not in the medium run nor in the long run. On the other hand, this situation does call for some sort of response on the part of the United States. Whether or not it should call for an adversarial sort of response, or a sanction-based response, is a matter it seems to me of dispute—that is—should be open for discussion. So that's what I would first of all seek to bring to this discussion, is just a remembrance of the wisdom of the ages, if you will.

Citations about Russia from U.S. presidents, through the ages: the United States of America was founded of course in, technically, 1783, 1787, and 1789 with the ratification of the U.S. Constitution, but it wasn't until—so let's take that point—OK, the ratification of the U.S. Constitution. It wasn't until several decades later that the Russian Empire recognized formally, diplomatically the United States, and it did so in 1809. But it was several years after that before the first reference to Russia in any presidential State of the Union was made, and that was done by James Madison. We can look at some of the patterns of relations to Russia over the long run in a few minutes here, but I'd like to begin with two citations from two presidents. And in the interest of balance, I've chosen a Democrat and a Republican.

OK. The first, a Democrat. This is Martin Van Buren, the eighth president of the United States of America, in his first annual State of the Union message, on December 5 of 1837. Here is what he had to say: "Between Russia and the United States, sentiments of good will continue to be mutually cherished. Our minister recently accredited to that court has been received with a frankness and cordiality and with evidences of respect for his country, which leave us no room to doubt the preservation in the future of those amicable and liberal relations which have so long and so interruptedly existed between the two countries. On the few subjects under discussion between us, an early and just decision is confidently anticipated." President Martin Van—Democratic President Martin Van Buren, eighth president of the United States.

So in the interest of partisan balance, I've selected as another superscript a citation from a Republican president, Mr. Ronald Reagan. Here's what he had to say in his address before a joint session of the Congress on the State of the Union on January 25, 1984.

Here's what Mr. Reagan had to say: "Tonight I want to speak to the people of the Soviet Union to tell them it's true that our governments have had serious differences. But our sons and daughters have never fought each other in war. If we Americans have our way, they never will. People of the Soviet Union, President Dwight Eisenhower, who fought by your side in World War II, said—quote—the essential struggle is not merely man against man or nation against nation; it is man against war. Americans—end of quote—Americans are people of peace. If your government wants peace, there will be peace. We can come together in faith and friendship to build a safer and far better world for our children and for our children's children, and the whole world will rejoice. That is my message to you." This is Ronald Reagan. I think everyone in this room understands that Ronald Reagan was no friend of Marxism-Leninism, he was no friend of communism, and yet he found a way to adopt this kind of a conciliatory disposition to the Soviet Union.

The third superscript that I have, and again, leading this work, is a citation from an ancient sacred text. I'll read it in the original language. (In foreign language—ancient Hebrew: Al-tasog gebul olam, asher ehso abotheka) And this is from the book of proverbs. And it said, "remove not an ancient landmark which your fathers have set." And it talked about a "gebul olam" in the original Hebrew; they weren't talking about a line of political boundary; they were talking about precedent. They were talking about practice. They were talking about a disposition that proved its validity in the course of time. OK. Again, if you'll indulge me, I'd like to read a couple paragraphs from the manuscript.

"Russia and the United States have enjoyed very good cooperative and productive relations for most of the years in which the United States of America has existed. This may come as a surprise to many Americans who perhaps instinctively regard Russia as a potential or actual adversary of our country. To be sure, the Cold War period from the latter 1940s until the latter 1980s marked an era of profound mutual distrust and no small amount of dislike between our countries. The Cold War era also involved episodes of indirect hostility in the form of proxy wars, as in Korea, Vietnam and several African countries, including Angola, Mozambique, Ethiopia, and arguably in other regions as well. These were proxy—these proxy wars were exorbitantly costly and bloody to each side. Viewed from a long-term historical perspective, however, the Cold War represents an anomaly and a deviation from the larger historical pattern of our relations with Russia. This is an important but often-overlooked fact in the history of our countries." And I would—I didn't put it in the text, but I'll add it here that if I dare say so, it's an element that, from my view, at least, personally, is deeply embedded in the American psyche, that there's something about Russia that is intrinsically adversarial to the United States, and viewed—certainly, viewed from the long-term perspective of U.S.-Russian relations, not only is it not true, but it's patently untrue, and an examination of those patterns over the long period becomes abundantly clear as we look at what our presidents had to say, to return to the text. [resumes citation of text:] "This will become clear as we look at the manner in which U.S. presidents refer to Russia and the Soviet Union in our annual State of the Union addresses." Article II, section III of the U.S. Constitution requires of the president that, quote, "he shall, from time to time, give to the Congress information on the state of the union, and recommend to their consideration such measures as he shall judge necessary and expedient." George Washington set the precedent of doing so annually, and in late autumn, although his first message to Congress was on January 8th of 1790. His next was on December of that year. Washington's first message was delivered orally, as were all of his subsequent messages to Congress, and those of his successor,

John Adams. Thomas Jefferson began the tradition of providing to the Congress an annual written message, quote, "on the State of the Union," with his first message in December 1801. All such messages followed suit until Woodrow Wilson's first annual message to Congress was delivered orally. Shortly after being elected president of the United States, Mr. Barack Obama signaled his intention to, quote, "reset America's relations with Russia," since those relations seemed to him, and so many other Americans, as having gone seriously awry as a result of the policies and practices of the previous presidency. The Russian government welcomed this intention and responded favorably to it. This study seeks to shed light on the long-range historical patterns of the U.S.' disposition to Russia as expressed in presidential State of the Union messages." There's nothing simple about U.S.-Russian relations, and yet, on the other hand, there's never been any direct hostility between the United States and Russia, and we hope that there won't be. What I hope in this discussion, that we can begin to do, is to begin to look at this entire situation that we've gotten ourselves into between the United States of America and the Russian Federation—perhaps, from the perspective of the other side, perhaps encourage the Russians—the leadership of the Russian Federation—to understand the concerns of the United States. A lot of words have flowed back and forth, and some have been, it seems to me, productive and constructive, other ones, perhaps, have not. But I would, if I may, just like to cite for a moment: there was an article that appeared a couple of days ago in the New Republic by Mr. Michael Kimmage. He mentions that this isn't the return of the Cold War—it's worse. And there's much in this article, frankly, that I find rather insightful in light of my own research here. Mr. Kimmage offers the following: He says the Cold War binaries—in other words, the images and the concepts from the Cold War that help us understand the situation now—the Cold War binaries cover up the most interesting binary to have emerged from Ukraine. Reacting to the same crisis—reacting to the same crisis, Putin and Obama have committed themselves to two irreconcilable visions of international politics. "In Mr. Putin's view, solidarity flows from the ethnos, from the language, religion and history of a particular people formed into a state. The rhythm of international politics is set by the assertion of power, and the international community is at best a fiction. In truth, it does not exist. Beyond it are states who participate in international affairs as they see fit. As emphasized, and never out of pure altruism, and least of all—least altruistic of all is the United States, according to this vision of the world, as emphasized in a Russian Foreign Ministry response to a March 5 State Department fact sheet on Ukraine. It says,—quote—from the Russian Foreign Ministry, "The U.S. does not and will never have the moral authority to teach others about international norms and respect to other countries' sovereignty. What about the bombings of former Yugoslavia and the invasion of Iraq on false pretenses?" End of citation. Mr. Kimmage continues. "In a rival vision, the international community and America's leading role within it is fully real. It has values that are real, and these values encourage democracy, rule of law, human rights and a free media. The "international community," quote, unquote, has recognized Ukraine's will to be a part of the international community. Over time, and with the help of the EU and the US, Ukraine will draw closer to the international community, until, one day, it exists seamlessly within it." This is the other vision. Kimmage's point is that these two visions are irreconcilable, and in that, I would tend to agree with him. It seems to me that if any sort of improvement of U.S.-Russian relations is going to occur, then what we need to do is, first of all, understand those two irreconcilable visions, and not so much figure out which one is right and which one is wrong, but look at where they came from, what validity might be—might exist in each one of these two visions, to begin building upon those points, building some sorts of bridges to arrive at a higher understanding, and therefore, at a more productive and durably useful way to relate to each other. As far as I'm concerned, if someone wants to understand—and again, I'm an American, I'm a—as you can tell from my last name, I'm a Slavic-derived—American; I'm kind of a "Heinz 57": I've got a little bit of everything in me. I'm not a Russian, and I don't pretend to come from within that culture—I do not. But it seems to me that if one wants to understand Russia and where Russia has been for the last 10 years or so under Mr. Putin's leadership, yeah, you can read the official statements and so on. But something I find particularly useful, and with this—well, actually, two things—I will close very, very briefly here. An article appeared—and I brought a copy with me—in the American journal called the Atlantic Monthly. This was in May of 2001. Mr. Putin had been President of Russia at that point for almost a year and a half. And the title of the article is "Russia is Finished: The Unstoppable Descent into Social Catastrophe and Strategic Irrelevance," written by Jeffrey Tayler. Eighteen pages—he goes on and on and on. The information in those pages is factually correct. Russia faced a daunting array, not only of problems that were residual from the USSR, but also, a daunting array of problems that had accumulated as a result of—let's just be polite about it—decisions that were made during the 1990s, both within Russia and abroad.

The point is that when Mr. Putin came into the presidency on January 1st of the year 2000, he had a lot of problems on his desk. There is no question about that. So much so and as you know, the Atlantic Monthly is not a hysterical media outlet—18 pages: he goes on and on. I'll cite one or two paragraphs, and that will close it. Here's what he said—listen to it. This perhaps will help us to understand where Russia is coming from in all this, in order to, in turn, put us in a position to begin building some of those bridges. Here's what Mr. Tayler had to say. "I have arrived at a conclusion." And he talks about how he studied Russia all his life, and he's lived there, and so on—"I arrived at a conclusion that is at odds with what I previously thought. Internal contradictions in Russia's thousand-year history have destined it to shrink demographically and weaken economically and possibly disintegrate territorially. The drama is coming to a close, and within a few decades, Russia will concern the rest of the world no more than any other third-world country with abundant resources, an impoverished people, and a corrupt government. In short, as a great power, Russia is finished."

He goes on for 18 pages to cite fact after fact after fact to support this conclusion of his, that, quote, "Russia is finished." And he concludes with these words: he says, "What does this mean for the Western world? It is difficult to imagine the birth of an ideological conflict between Russia and the West similar to that which led to the Cold War." He would agree with Kimmage. "The Russian nationalist sentiments are likely to increase," and they most surely have since May of 2001, when this was published, "and to find expression in ever-more bellicose pronouncements from the Kremlin, especially if the West and NATO persist in humiliating Moscow with military adventures in their former spheres of influence. Otherwise, to the benefit of the Russian elite, Western business will continue to operate in the havens of Moscow and St. Petersburg, where investment, both Russian and foreign, will ensure a well-maintained infrastructure." "As regions deteriorate within Russia," Tayler offered, "these two cities are likely to continue developing and growing. Moscow's population officially stands at 9 million, but may actually be as high as 12 million. Western governments will continue to buy cheap Russian oil and gas,"—this was written in 2001, and they certainly have—"and will quite possibly invest heavily in the upkeep of these industries. As for superpower status, in contrast to the Turks, under Kemal Ataturk, who voluntarily relinquished their empire in favor of an Anatolian homeland, or the Byzantine Greeks, who fell in the battle defending their empire against the Turks, the Russians are likely to face a slow, relatively peaceful decline into obscurity, a process that is well underway."

Well, if I was a Russian, I would have been pretty insulted by that, but I would have been moved, I think, to do something about the realities that prompted that article in the first place. It seems to me that might be a good place to begin our discussion of how to go about rebuilding relations with the Russian Federation. Thank you very much.

Mr. PARKER. Thank you, Jim, for that context. In order to keep things moving along, I want to spare any comments I have on the matter and turn it over immediately to Matt. Matt—sort of give us a wrap up—contemporary relevance—what is to be done? Where do we go from here? So good to have you with us today, Matt.

Mr. ROJANSKY. Got it. Thank you. Yeah, pleased to be here. Thank you, Kyle, for organizing this. Thanks, Representative Aderholt for joining us and thanks to all of you for coming. Obviously, it's an important topic at an important time. So actually, Jim set me up very well just before he went to the Atlantic—by all measures, a very thoughtful and interesting, but fundamentally, a sort of a pop publication, I suppose, by reminding us that we've got to go to primary sources, and we've got to do our research, and we've got to remember history. I've responded to what I think is an unsurprising tendency, but I think nonetheless a troubling tendency to fetishize everything that goes on in Mr. Putin's brain and in his life and his experience until, essentially, everything becomes about the Putin story, whether you think he's Darth Vader, or whether you think he's the second coming of Peter the Great, or whether you think he's something else, everything becomes about Mr. Putin. For the people who are so preoccupied with Mr. Putin, they often spend very little time paying attention to what Mr. Putin says and why he says it. He's often quite clear about what he believes and why. So one of the many illuminating Putin speeches and articles that I was inspired to go back to, by the speech of his that I listened to last week—and I encourage all those of you who understand Russian, listen to it in the original on YouTube; it's incredible. This is the speech to a joint session of the Duma and the Federation Council about why, in fact, Russia is taking Crimea, and what happens next.

But I went back to his 2007 Munich speech—now famous—but again, I think famous in a lot of circles that folks—most of whom have not actually read the speech or listened to it. So he says the following: "We are seeing a greater and greater disdain for the basic principles of international law. And independent legal norms are, as a matter of fact, coming increasingly closer to one state's legal system. One state, and of course, first and foremost, the United States, has overstepped its national borders in every way. This is visible in the economic, political, cultural and educational policies it imposes on other nations. Who likes this? Who's happy about this?

In international relations, we increasingly see the desire to resolve questions according to so-called issues of political expediency based on current politics—current political climate. This is extremely dangerous. It results in the fact that no one feels safe. I want to emphasize this: No one feels safe, because no one can feel that international law is like a stone wall that will protect them. Of course, such a policy stimulates an arms race.

And he goes on, and then finally says, I'm convinced that we have reached that decisive moment when we must seriously think about the architecture of global security."

Now, I think the reason that these lines are important is not only that it demonstrates Mr. Putin's dissatisfaction, the fact that he gives quite rhetorically powerful speeches, but the appeal that he is making here for the primacy of international law not on behalf of Russia and Russia's interests—which he insists in the course of the rest of the speech Russia has—unique, independent—particularly foreign policy interests—that will not be sacrificed to any other country, not least of all the United States. But then he says specifically: Who—who in the world, no other country, could possibly be comfortable with this state of affairs. Indeed we need to go back to first principles in order to strengthen the international system. But what I found interesting as I reviewed others of Mr. Putin's speeches and his deeds was that, in the ensuing years, I get the sense that his perspective turned around 180 degrees. His feeling was rather than reform the international system, rather than try to shore up what he felt were international rules that were under attack, it might be better simply to advance Russia's national interest in much the way the United States, in his view, had done over the preceding decade or decade and a half without regard to these ostensible international rules, which the United States, first and foremost, among many other countries, had demonstrated that they didn't take seriously anyway.

You see a progression of this here beginning during Munich 2007, Moscow 2011 when, again, Mr. Putin's perspective was that the United States was intervening in what should have been sacrosanct, and that is Russia's domestic political process—the Duma elections, the presidential elections in which Mr. Putin returned to the Kremlin. Finally, this year Sochi 2014, when even an international humanitarian event; that is, international brotherhood and sporting competition, became simply an opportunity for the West the United States again, first and foremost—to malign, expose, attack and ultimately isolate Mr. Putin, even though in his view he had done whatever might have been needed, including releasing political prisoners, to facilitate a more neutral approach to what is, after all, a shared global opportunity, the Olympic Games.

So what does all this mean? It means that if Mr. Putin starts from a premise that there is a sense of injustice, a sense of dishonesty and disingenuousness in which the international community as a whole now looks at international law and rules, that in fact not only are there no rules—functionally there are no reliable rules of the game—but there is no trust. There is no foundation on which to rebuild those rules.

That's particularly troubling, I think, in the context here of the Helsinki Commission, when we're thinking about the Organization for Security and Cooperation in Europe, to which, I think wisely, we have attempted to turn in dealing with the Ukraine crisis, needing some foundation, something that is inclusive, something that is perceptive, something that can bring a little bit of clarity to what's going on, on the ground. If you understand Mr. Putin's position today as being that there is no trust, that there is no fundamental mutual understanding around these rules, that is, in fact, very troubling.

But of course our task—and this is, again, where I take issue with the pure preoccupation with Putin—is not to heal Mr. Putin of his psychology, nor is it to heal Russia of Putin or of "Putinism." But nor is it to achieve some kind of grand victory in a struggle of good versus evil in the world in which Putin conveniently plays the role of Darth Vader. Our task is instead to advance the American national interest and to do so according to rational principles. How, given this premise that I have sketched, might we do that in the current environment? What, for example, might President Obama's next State of the Union address, to the extent he wishes to talk about Russia, include? I think four basic principles.

The first is we have to communicate with Russians. When I say that, I mean all Russians. Here is where I don't entirely disagree with the administration's policy, which for a very long time has called for a dual-track approach. To the extent that that means talking to the Russian leadership but also talking to Russian society, I think it makes a lot of sense. But, very importantly, we cannot allow others to be our interlocutors. And this happens far too often, whether those others are the Ukrainians, the Georgians, the Russian political opposition, or the Kremlin itself. Very often when you talk to Russians, which I do all the time, you find that they have not heard Americans describe what Americans want. They've heard someone else—it's been filtered through some other perspective, and that gives them a false idea of what we are and what we're after.

Second, I think we have to define very concrete interests that are commensurate with our still considerable political, economic and military power in the world. And I think we need to talk to Russians specifically about those interests that concern them. And more often than not, those are interests that fall in the post-Soviet space. This is a concept with which we have been consistently uncomfortable. You know, President Obama I think disclaims this from the very first moment in every one of his speeches by saying there's no such thing as spheres. This is an outdated concept—spheres of influence, spheres of privileged interest—that the reality is, as seen from Russia's perspective, the post-Soviet space is a distinctive neighborhood in which Russia has distinctive interests.

In order to talk to the Russians effectively, I think we have to acknowledge that fact. But nonetheless, our top priorities are clearly going to remain issues like resolving the Iran nuclear situation, North Korea, Afghanistan, and I think we need to have very clear and concrete asks of the Russians in these areas rather than what I think too often we have done, which is to come to the table with abstractions, ideas about what, in theory, ought to be good for the world or what in theory ought to be good for Russia, right: Russia could turn around its problems if only it would adhere to this particular set of principles. And again, if you accept the premise that I began from, I think the Russian leadership at this point has moved beyond those principles, does not accept that there's any legitimacy or trust left as a foundation for them.

I think the third point—I sort of moved my third and fourth point—stem from the idea that if we are fundamentally concerned about what has happened in Ukraine today, the best revenge is living well, right? I think it supplies, in an international relations context, almost better than it does in personal life, because here revenge, rather than being satisfying, is likely to be truly disastrous. So I think we need to develop and protect the tool kit that we have begun—very slowly but steadily—to deploy in response to the Russian action in Crimean, and that's fundamentally an economic tool kit. But on what is that tool kit premised, right? We're far more likely to use sanctions at any point in the rest of the 21st century than we are guns, bombs, nuclear weapons, what have you. Those really are the tools of the 20th century.

So the calls to double down on 20th century weapons and tools I think are misguided, but I think in order to support the economic levers that we are in fact using and are going to use, but which today are in their infancy—they're like World War I fighter planes.

Who knows how to use them? The Europeans acknowledge freely that they don't really know how to use them yet, and that's part of the reason why you haven't seen them effectively deployed.

Mr. PARKER. The sanctions technology.

Mr. ROJANSKY. The sanctions technology, that's right. It's in its infancy. And so to effectively support it, I think we have to insist on a scenario where the benefits for participation in what has been fundamentally a Western-led global economic system outweigh the costs. Here I think we're at a vital inflection point, because in having imposed I think quite significant—and increasingly significant if you look at the third executive order that's come out, which I think has not yet been fully fleshed out in implementation—sanctions against the biggest economy that we have ever sanctioned. It's bigger than the added-up GDPs of any every other economy that the United States has ever imposed sanctions on—Belarus, Burma, Iran, Cuba, down the line. But the implication of this is that those who are on the periphery of this international system, or who are in it but wonder about their relationship with the United States, with Washington, with Brussels in the future, may have doubts about whether being fully subject to that system going forward is in their interest. Then the priority needs to be on successes like TTIP, for example, ensuring that the Trans-Atlantic economic relationship, that the economic system in which the United States does have a vital role of leadership—think about dollar-based transactions, right? To clear a dollar transaction you basically have to go through the United States, with a few limited exceptions. The idea that that system is of more benefit to those who take part in it than it is of cost, because of politics, is vitally important to having the tool kit we need to have going forward. Then finally, on this theme of living well, I think in Ukraine specially we're also at an inflection point. We may be at risk of missing the big picture, and that is that the long-term victory in Ukraine comes from the success of Ukraine. It doesn't come from the precise shape of Ukraine's borders. This is not an attempt to whitewash Crimea. I think we need to persistently object on that point, as we have on any of the other post-Soviet conflicts. But it comes from the idea that the Ukrainians effectively developed the institutions of liberal democracy and market prosperity that they had, after almost 25 years in the post-Soviet area, failed to do thus far.

I think my concern here is, while we're giving plenty of love, political love, to the new Ukrainian leadership, interim leadership—and we will probably continue to do so before, during and after the May presidential elections—we may fail to give the tough love that is necessary to ensure that precisely the conditions the Ukrainians have negotiated—for example, most recently with the IMF; and I'm very pleased to see that, or under the previous government with the EU for the association agreement—that those conditions are now punted down the road and that the politics and the embrace comes first.

That would be fundamentally mistaken, because here is where we need to insist on the difficult steps that ultimately lead to Ukraine's success, because this, in the end, denies the victory scenario for those who would like to see Ukraine dismembered, and that is post-Soviet twilight. You cannot live in post-Soviet darkness if you're participating fully in the European system and the global economic system. So I think I'll end right there.

Mr. PARKER. Thank you, Matt. Thank you for that summation.

We've spoken at you for now 40 minutes. I'd like to get the conversation going right away. Feel free: questions, comments, objections, points, counterpoints. Please, the floor is yours, and we're on the record. No one? Oh, please. Right here. And if you could—if you don't mind saying who you are, we'd love to have it in the record.

QUESTIONER. Yeah, Steve Traber Congressman Pearce's staff. Actually, from my seat I see the map there, and my question is more along the lines of something semi-superficial.

We hear a lot about the concern of the periphery countries who have either Russian majorities or substantial Russian minorities. Has anyone ever seen a map that—a demographic map that actually lays out, you know, how many are in the Balkan states, how many are in Kazakhstan? I mean, where does Putin's eye wander when he looks at the map, since he obviously knows where they're at? As a general statement, should those places be concerned with his philosophy, as you have so well laid out?

Mr. WARHOLA. Well, I'll make some comments on that and then Matt can correct, embellish as may be necessary.

Mr. PARKER. I'm going to do my best to keep this rapid fire so we get through a lot of questions.

Mr. WARHOLA. Sure, and I will try to be brief. Very, very good question. Thank you very much. Thank you once again for coming.

When the Soviet Union collapsed in 1991, there were, nobody knows exactly how many, ethnic Russians—and again, that—as you know, the definition of an ethnic Russian is a little bit fuzzy. Some of it's self-defined. The figure that's often given, and that was by the Russian government and by others, was about 30 million Russians living in the former Soviet territories but outside of the boundaries of the Russian Federation itself—about 30 million.

Some of those ended up, moving to Russia. And I won't say "back to Russia", because some of them had been in those territories such as, Turkmenistan, and through the Baltic areas—some of them had been there for generations. And so there was no idea of moving "back to Russia" because, you know, they had been in those territories for generations, but about 30 million. Some did go "back" to Russia.

In fact, there were a series of policies pursued by the Russian government in the latter 1990s, and then given increased impetus in the 2000s under President Putin, to bring more and more of them back to Russia and—or back into Russia. Some came, but not as many as the Russian government would have hoped.

The major pockets of ethnic Russians outside of the Russian Federation but in the former Soviet republics, there are certainly more than a few of them in Latvia, which, as you know, of course is a NATO and EU member. In the eastern portion of Moldova and the Transnistria region——

Mr. PARKER. Kazakhstan?

Mr. WARHOLA. Kazakhstan is the next in the northern part—Kazakhstan is composed of 20 oblasts, including the capital city, or 20 regions. The three northern oblasts, or regions, of Kazakhstan are very large. Kazakhstan is an enormously large country, as you can see on the map. The three northern regions, or states if we could call them in the American context, have close to, or in one or two cases, a majority of ethnic Russians living there as well.

In some of the other former Soviet countries—Azerbaijan, for example—they figure it's about, maybe a few percent, 5 percent of the population is Russian, although I was in Baku a few years ago and one hears, right, about one out of every three people on the streets of Baku speak Russian. Some of them are obviously Russian just by the physiognomy and so on. So, you know, I suspect there's more than 5 percent of them there.

Mr. PARKER. I would just quickly add that Kazakhstan, among some others, like Ukraine, relinquished its nuclear arsenal——

Mr. WARHOLA. Right.

Mr. PARKER [continuing]. Supported and encouraged by the United States, lauded as a great success. The Nunn-Lugar Cooperative Threat Reduction Program, we funded that, here in this building.

Other questions? Please.

Mr. WARHOLA. There was—I'm sorry; there was a lady back there whose hand went up simultaneously with the gentleman's.

Mr. PARKER. Yeah, I'm sorry. We'll take two—two, three in a row. Alexei and then we'll move right through. Yep, please. If you could just say your name for the record, you can stand so everybody can hear.

QUESTIONER. I'm a private citizen basically, representing, here, myself. What I would like to say is that—I'd like to make a segue between what——

Mr. PARKER. Can you identify your name for the record?

QUESTIONER. Alexei Sobchenko

Mr. PARKER. OK, Alexei Sobchenko.

QUESTIONER. The segue is the following: To say—to speak about ethnic Russians is like to speak about ethnic Americans. Anybody who speaks Russian can be. And going back to what Mr. Rojansky said, is basically—the message was that Ukrainians are supposed to become adults and start to act—if I'm—I'm making synopsis—supposed to start like adults and take responsibility for themselves and to blame anybody else for whatever happens to them.

The funny thing is that I'm an ethnic Ukrainian. And I'm exactly what you call ethnic Russian because my native tongue is Russian and I can be as much Russian as I am Ukrainian. For that point of view, Russians and Ukrainians are basically the same nation. The only difference is that Russians have oil, Ukrainians don't.

The result of this whole diversion, why Ukraine is so rambunctious and rioting and Russians are not is because Ukrainians have no oil. Russians are as much of a dysfunctional nation as Ukraine is, which is kind of glossed up with—glossed over with oil and gas revenues. And if we continue the same logic about Ukraine, that Ukrainians should start to make up their minds, and said, well, basically stop finger pointing at whose fault is—you know, why there is such a mess.

The same could be true about Russia. And from that point of view, jumping back to what we started with, is that these sanctions—no matter how painful, no matter how unpleasant and how unreasonable one can present them in the context of this history of U.S.-Russian relationships, could do a certain good, could make Russians face the reality, which for a long, long time they were ignoring thanks to the oil revenues.

If one looks at Putin's speech, which I did, early on he asserts that Belarus, Ukraine and Russia share not only religion—which is orthodoxy, which he states very firmly.

Therefore, they share a civilization, culture and human rights. Therefore, it seems to me that one can make the argument that he is going to international law, yes, but pre-Westphalia Treaty of the 17th century, which looks at the basis of comity or, I guess, sovereignty as religious. So can you comment on that?

Mr. PARKER. Matt, you want to take that quick and then Jim for a follow-up? And then we'll move on.

Mr. ROJANSKY. Yeah, he does say that. You're talking about the speech last week? What's interesting is he says also some fundamentally 20th century things. So he talks about Crimea, for example, that be the Crimea of Russians, of Ukrainians, of Crimean Tatars, right, and will always be the Crimea of the Russian Federation, right?

He is absolutely asserting a role as protector of the Rus, right, and uniter of Russia's historical lands, gatherer of the lands, person who solved the time of troubles that was described in The Atlantic article. Yet the same time, he's still touching on these themes of kind of rule of law, protection of minorities. He defines democracy in terms of majority role, with consideration for minorities needs and so on.

I think the answer here is he is in the process of turning around on what had maybe a decade ago been a desire to reassert the primacy of rules as a way of keeping this adventurism by everyone but Russia down. He now sees some benefits to adventurism by Russia, right, whether it's the Eurasian Union or its Crimea specifically or it's Transnistria or something else. I think in that context he needs to reorient his position on the rules.

Whether it's going back to a pre-Westphalian notion of statehood as being based on nationality or it's using—and for example, he used the concept—of diaspora, right? He defined Russia post-1991, the Russians as being sudden Europe's biggest diaspora, with 30 million or something else, right? So he's aligning and mixing a lot of concepts here. I think it's reflecting—again, not to do psychoanalysis—but I think it's a reorientation, if you go back to 2007 at least.

Probably there are some speeches before that, of what had been a relatively clear-cut position that said there's the U.N. Charter and there shouldn't be anything else. And you all are not respecting the U.N. Charter. He is now looking for other options because clearly there's no trust left in that institution.

Mr. WARHOLA. An interesting question and I guess—I don't know, as an academic it immediately called to mind, you know, Samuel Huntington's image of the global map in terms of, in the—into the 21st century of, as you know, the clash of civilizations. And according to Professor Huntington, one of the most important dividing lines would be the line between the West and the Orthodox civilizations.

Does this kind of validate Dr. Huntington's point of view? Well, I'm not sure. But it—there does seem to be a pretty clear and sharp dividing line in terms of the nature of the relationship between the state and the underlying society, between the Orthodox lands and the lands that find themselves to their—to their west. Is it our obligation to try and put pressure on them to change, to make them us—more like us? I don't know. I find useful some of the insights of Lilia Shevtsova's 2010 book. It's called—perhaps in a title that was almost prescient—it's called "Lonely Power," why Russia is not the West and why the West, doesn't understand Russia—or something like that—something to that effect—but the main title is "The Lonely Power."

Mr. PARKER. Before we move on, I want to recognize Don Jensen and thank him for coming. Don is with the Center for Transatlantic Relations at SAIS, Johns Hopkins, and the author of one of the articles we distributed, "Can the U.S. and Russia Ever get Along?" Don just wrote a day or ago, and it was out on the table, a wonderful review of Angela Stent's recent book, and he called it a magisterial work on U.S.-Russia relations and Don is a veteran of embassy Moscow. Don, you have some comment, question, anything that you can offer to us?

QUESTIONER. I want to dive in the middle of a very interesting discussion. I have a couple points. My friend's comment about the commonality of blood between Ukrainians and Russians, I just want to make sure that for me, one of the lessons of the current crisis is that—how much Ukrainians' values are not Russian. The entire Ukrainian crisis for me, since November, has shown the importance of values, not pure realism in international relations. But Ukrainians' values are not interested in blood, are different to a significant extent than many Russians. I don't want to generalize about political culture, but I think it accounts for some of the difference in behavior.

Cathy, I agree with you. One of the things about the speech that struck me was the extent to which Putin, and compared to the past, uses the phrase rossisskii—ruski, not rossisskii, indicating ethnic kinship. If this is going to be a driving force in Russian views towards the whatever country might have ethnic Russians. And I'm from former Russian California, but perhaps the only Italian who speaks Russian in Sonoma County. But this is a very destabilizing force. And that is probably why they talked about the importance of membership in international institutions for the first Putin epoch. Now they don't. And they talked about the importance of international institutions in Syria and Iran, the importance of nonintervention. Well, now they've turned that upside down, on I think very questionable ethnic grounds.

My final point would be that in general, and not applicable anybody in particular, there is a tendency I think to blame the victim, Ukraine, here much more—in the debate about the Ukraine—much more than we should. We certainly should blame them—the government's horrible and impotent and all those other things. But the tough love, or just tough—ought to be applied to Russia as well, because I think there is a double standard here. A lot of the first Obama term was sort of entranced by the idea of a lot of realism in great power dealing with Russia, not these little Ukraines and other countries in the near-abroad, which I think frankly sounded to me very patronizing. Ukraine is a country of 50 million people almost. It's a vital strategic asset to not—to both Europe and Russia and I think over the long term I would be hopeful that some accommodation could be reached.

But I think we have to start questioning the assumptions we tend to bring to this discussion, one of which is that Ukraine is not just a pet of Mother Russia. Ukraine is a separate country with—to a significant extent a different language and a considerably different culture. I think we ought to treat it with a little bit more seriousness.

Mr. PARKER. Thank you, Don. Jim, very briefly, and then we're going to go to the other side of the room.

Mr. WARHOLA. Yeah, just an additional comment real, real quickly, yeah, to Cathy's point once again. I mean, as far as I'm concerned, your point is well-taken. The referendum that was held in Crimea, I don't think it's an accident that the—that the Crimean Tatars boycotted that en mass. You know, the ballot—it was printed in first of all Russian, secondly Ukrainian, thirdly in Tatar.

Some of my research involved, Russian-Turkish relations and that—and the kind of tangle, or the relation—the triangle—Russia, Turkey, the Crimean Tatars—is an interesting one. If we had time we could get into it; we can't. But you know, I just wanted to say that, on the one hand, I agree with Matt—it was mentioned in the speech—not particularly—with any particular force. But, you know, the point is well-taken. I don't think it's an accident, they appear to me to have just been—just kind of steamrolled, for lack of a better word.

Mr. PARKER. Thank you. This side please.

QUESTIONER. I'm from the—Library of Congress. My one small remark actually—Georgians are as well, but it didn't bother Putin to go to war with Georgia, with an nation. The second, I would like to ask Mr. Rojansky to clarify your predictions about the Ukrainian government succession. I mean, having in mind the fact that current government officials are the part of the Tymoshenko team mainly, which were not less corrupted than the previous government. And they developed a system which, you know, just brought down Ukraine and left Crimea to the Russians. So what do you think about it? There are several criminal cases in different countries against them. Thank you.

Mr. PARKER. Matt.

Mr. ROJANSKY. Yeah. First of all, I didn't pretend to offer predictions. That's a great way to be wrong. I don't like that. But what I would say—I think—you know, you're right—you're right to an extent about the current team being the Tymoshenko team, but there's a bit of a change underway. I do think—I get the sense that Yatsenyuk is for, frankly, probably personal ambition kinds of reasons trying to distance himself from Tymoshenko and, to the extent that she still controls the party, from the party. I think he expects to continue to serve as prime minister, whoever is president after May.

QUESTIONER. But she knows she is going to be the president——

Mr. ROJANSKY. She may not be. I mean, she's not actually all that popular. I think the one thing she has going for her, and this really is where I think it is strongly incumbent on the United States and on the European Union not to allow the Ukrainians to play a game with us that they have played very effectively for 20 years, which is the Russian boogeyman, ignore everything else—you know, ignore every other problem because this problem is so overwhelming.

Now, unfortunately, the Crimean crisis has handed them the strongest possible argument. From Georgia, you should know, right, that that's exactly what the Georgian territory did for Saakashvili for a decade, right, was it handed him an argument that trumped very other argument. We only saw—when the elections came and we just how dirty and horrible things had become on live video—or, not live, but, you know, very visible in front of our faces.

Do we have to wait for another raft of evidence about thievery, corruption and corporate raiding in Ukraine to believe that the old guard is really, really filthy? I don't think so. I think—again, I don't have any great faith in individuals in Ukraine, by the way. I mean, anybody who's asking who is the great white hope for Ukraine's future is asking the wrong pronoun. It's not who; it's what. It's what institutions are going to transform Ukraine.

I want to give credit where it's due. I spent two months as a fellow with the U.S. embassy in Kiev thanks to Title 8, a program which, on the record, I would like to say should be fully restored, because it is vitally important for our understanding of this region. I saw on the ground how U.S. assistance, over a three-year period, had fundamentally transformed the prosecutorial system in Ukraine, which has finally now got a new law in place that could actually change the prosecutor's power to intervene in political cases, that's the tool. That's the tool that the executive branch uses to get its outcomes wherever it wants, as well as the judicial reforms.

You know, so focusing on institutions in that way now—that's what I meant by tough love. It wasn't to blame the Ukrainians, Don I mean, the idea is to focus on the hard steps, and maybe not even everything in the association agreement, because it's huge, but that's a wonderful road map. Pick three, four, five of the biggest-ticket items. Those will be the things that dictate a successful outcome. So if you want me to make a prediction, the prediction is this: If you can get several of those in place and locked down now and you can use the IMF money that's just been unleashed as well as the U.S. loan guarantee and the European money to do it, then I think Ukraine actually will be a success, you know, whoever gets elected in May. And I frankly don't care very much about that.

Mr. PARKER. Thank you. Next question. I saw you first. Sorry.

QUESTIONER. Hi, Nina Jankowicz, National Democratic Institute for International Affairs. I have three quick points. First, Matt, thanks for bringing up Title 8. I think many of us in this room have benefited from Title 8, including myself, and I would wholeheartedly like to voice my support for its reinstatement. The other two points deal with the aid going to Ukraine and Russia right now. I just want to make sure that we sustain the aid going to Ukraine. It's great that we are bringing it up now that there's a crisis, but I don't want to see it go the route that it went in 1992 and in the early '90s. It needs to be more of a Poland situation and not a repeat of history.

On that same note, there are a lot of Russian activists and NGOs suffering right now under intense scrutiny from the Russian government, and we need to make sure that we're supporting them, in addition to those outside of Russia.

Mr. PARKER. Thank you for the comment. Question? Comments and questions are welcome, please. I welcome both.

QUESTIONER. Bishkek initiative You would not equalize United Kingdom of Great Britain—not an island with British and you would not equalize Austria with Austria and Hungary why do you equalize Russian Federation with USSR and Russian Empire?

Mr. PARKER. Good question for Jim.

QUESTIONER. It is—it is independent state, which formed only a part of the Soviet Union and Russian Empire, but they are not equal.

Mr. WARHOLA. Sure, of course.

Mr. PARKER. So I guess, Jim, they're not equal, but how much does the history weigh on it going forward, and particularly with—I know you might argue that the Cold War is something of an aberration. So are we snipping that out and connecting history back to the imperial line, as if the Cold War had—as if that German experiment had never happened?

Mr. WARHOLA. My own particular study was the study of U.S. presidents' relation with first the Russian Empire and then with the USSR and then—the Russian Federation; U.S. president referred to the Soviet Union as the Soviet Union until Franklin Delano Roosevelt did in 1945.

Mr. PARKER. He didn't refer to it much at all, right?

Mr. WARHOLA. Once, yeah. No, not at all. You know, and—but it was considered by presidents, at least as reflected in their State of the Union addresses, as coterminous with Russia. We know of course that's, as you know, not exactly correct, but that's the way it was—it was seen by them. I'm not sure if that's much of an answer, but—and no, I certainly understand that, as you know, Ireland is not England and that Austria is not Hungary and so on.

Mr. PARKER. Tonyayou brought up the Magnitsky Act. I had a quick point, and possibly a question, on sanctions technology, perhaps to you, Matt, something that's close to my heart. I saw the other day some comments—and I think they were almost being made as if the sanctions were—as if we had discovered some problem with the sanctions, that in fact they were helping Putin's nationalization of the elite. My view is, hey, we finally stumbled on a win-win. We have finally stumbled on something that helps get dirty money out of the West and into Russia. Russia's experienced capital flight. So why is it a bad thing, apart from the isolation of Russia that's coming anyway, that we clear our accounts of corrupt Russian money? I certainly don't mean that in an ethnic sense. To be fair, because one of the things I'm concerned about is if and when the Maidan or the revolution comes to Moscow, at some point the West—our rule of law—we may be forced to defend some unsavory people and keep them and their assets safe from the mob in Moscow, and I'm wondering how that can possibly inflame anti-American sentiment, that once again the dirty West is holding Russia's wealth and won't return it to the people who have sent it abroad and who might view their future, their families and others and have an exit strategy?

Mr. ROJANSKY. I mean, look, the whole complex of sanctions technology issues is fascinating, and especially when you add into it the question of the political impact and the sort of appearance effects of sanctions.

I take your point, Kyle, but I tend to think we have—so let me just answer it by analogy. If what you're arguing for is a kind of cleaner separation, you know, an approach where we can more easily sit on our side of the line, on our side of the trenches, and you know, shoot our artillery and know that it's at least hitting the stuff we want to hit over there, the answer is kind of, well, then you'd probably object to drone warfare, you know, special operations, intelligence and information warfare, sort of the realities that this is the 21st century. I think that sanctions technology success is actually going to be about understanding in much subtler and quieter ways how we achieve—for example, the dollar-clearing transaction or the euro-clearing transaction phenomenon is something that is often not about identifying particular assets, freezing them and appearing to do the things that are very costly, like for example, when it looks to Russians as if we're creating lists of good guys and bad guys, then we really play into the Kremlin's line that all we care about is regime change; all we care about is picking winners and losers in other countries; look at our sanctions list to see who we think are the good guys and who are the bad guys. One of the ways this has backfired in Belarus, for example, is that Lukashenko basically takes the list, he takes the EU list and the U.S. list, and he goes, all right, well, these people are all loyal, clearly, and all the rest of them, I'm going to cut them loose, right?

I think at the end of the day, what we need is the equivalent of, you know, a Stuxnet bomb, something that is smarter than the system altogether, that they don't figure out until it's too late that it was in fact our sanctions weapon that screwed them, but that the economy is getting hit, and it's getting hit in ways that hurt them more than it hurts us, because until that point, all we can do is kind of the old-fashioned legion against legion warfare, which is we are willing to endure more pain than you are, so we'll win on sanctions. And I think unfortunately, Putin is probably right that we're not willing to endure as much pain as he is because he's able to drag the Russian economy down as low as he wants, I mean, with limits, right, but we're certainly not willing to go, you know, scrape the bottom with him.

There's the danger of the backfire, too where it's—or those sort of sanctions—would just end up inadvertently strengthening his hand domestically.

Mr. PARKER. Well, and as you had mentioned in Belarus, so in Russia with some of these proposals, and we've seen them before after the Magnitsky Act, whereby the government says it will reimburse anyone for anything that's frozen or anything like that, and it's—to me, it's a sick irony, in a sense, that some of the money we've traced was actually stolen from Russia in the first place, so it gets to be stolen from Russia in the second place as it was reimbursed, because if and when we see such money, one of the options is that it is ultimately returned to the Russian treasury in a proper transaction.

Other questions, please? Inna Dubinsky.

QUESTIONER. Yes, Broadcasting Board of Governors. I actually am glad, Kyle, that you have turned the discussion from reactive options to more proactive, something that could, in the policies of the U.S. and its partners, tone down these territorial and other ambitions outside of Russian realm and scope.

Mr. PARKER. Thank you.

QUESTIONER. So just wanted to ask, what would be other policies, moves, ideas that could help that?

Mr. PARKER. Can we take one more question—let's take these together.

QUESTIONER. Yeah, this is actually on that note. There was an article on March——

Mr. PARKER. Yeah. Could——

QUESTIONER. I'm Marko Ceperkovic Congressman Alcee Hastings.

Mr. PARKER. Marco Jobelkovich yeah, Congressman Alcee Hastings' office.

QUESTIONER. So there was an article it was a European journal, maybe Der Spiegel. It was talking about the alternatives to the sanctions, because Germany is having—today Der Spiegel published that 50 percent of the Germans can kind of see the Russian position and limitedly agree to it and support Angela Merkel's neutrality—situation. So it's kind of worrying, but then on the other hand, it raises the question of alternatives to the sanctions, and would some other approaches be more of For example, should we not be trying to—and failing to punish those leaders while also punishing the people and maybe approach the people and a little bit of domestic issues? For example, there is a call for visa liberalization, because the European Union stopped visa liberalization. Maybe that would be more beneficial than actually cutting the visas and actually letting the ordinary people.

Mr. PARKER. Right, visa liberalization for nonservice passport holders. Exactly the opposite of what was being proposed. I appreciate the question because I would just underscore that as this Congress worked through personal sanctions in the context of the Magnitsky Act, at the same time, we supported of the visa liberalization that was happening concurrently the three-year agreements and whatever, sending a strong message that of course—broader contact, the door to America is open for those of good will who want to visit for legitimate purposes, but it is closing and we're drawing a harder line on the corruption front, human rights abuses, acknowledging that they often go hand in hand, that there's often a monetary component, and hardening our system to that.

Mr. ROJANSKY. I agree on the visa thing, and obviously I have many good friends in the State Department, not one of whom, no matter how many beers I pump into them, has given me a successful, like, rhetorically defensible answer as to why we can't have visa-free travel with Russia. It's not like we can't stop mobsters from coming in the country, and we do that—you know, we have visa-free with plenty of countries, and we stop criminals.

But on the question of, like, what other strategies might be deployed, I think there's one basic strategy, which kind of—I see Moldova, Ukraine and Russia existing on a spectrum of having figured this out. The Moldovan government three years ago finally realized that the only way to overcome the problem of Russian occupation in Transnistria was to make Moldova such a success story that the basis for that occupation, which is that Transnistrians are afraid of being reunited with Moldova and thereby sucked into Romania and Europe and all these horrible things, but they're no longer afraid of that.

The point is if you make Moldova fundamentally such a prosperous and successful part of the global economy, institutions that people can actually rely on to start businesses instead of to steal the businesses from them, then I think the position of Transnistrians, who are pretty much tired of having a government that steals everything from them, even though they get, you know, what is it—40 percent of them are pensioners, and they get nice, you know, Russian pensions if they accept Russian passports and so on. Fundamentally, it shifts the balance, right? By definition, the pensioners are not going to be around forever.

Again, with Ukraine, that gets harder because they start from the worst position, and the government doesn't understand that yet. Then in Russia itself, I think ultimately, that's the argument. It's not about defeating Russia; it's about integrating Russia into the global economy. I think that the United States has basically understood this. The problem is it's really hard to do, and it comes in fits and starts. It took us 17 years to get WTO, and look where we are now, right? So it's going to take a really long time. This is why—anybody asked me three years ago, or anybody talked to me three years ago, and I talked about Moldova, Transnistria, this, that and the other thing—I think I even testified about it. People just said, oh, who cares; it's Moldova. No, this is why the small post-Soviet countries matter, because they are test cases for these ideas. I think if you make it work right in Moldova, which the EU is very close to doing, then I think you do have a model.

Mr. WARHOLA. Sure, yeah. You know, on March 8th of this year—there was an editorial by Kasparov in The Wall Street Journal. What he advocated was very, very powerful sanctions, but sanctions not in general—but specifically targeting the Russian oligarchs. And his question was—why punish 140 million Russians when you've got a handful of oligarchs who are supporting Putin? Why not just pinpoint them? And you know, it's an interesting point of view.

In terms of sanctions, I mean, I don't know. I'm more of an historian-oriented student of Russian affairs than I am a—a political economist. I'm certainly not an economist, but I wonder about sanctions. It seems to me that, on the one hand, the United States has some obligation to object to the way in which the annexation of Crimea occurred, at the very least. The efficacy of sanctions, you know—I don't know. It makes me wonder: what are we after, with sanctions? What are we after? Are we out to punish Russia? Is that what we're after? And if so, why? And what do we hope to gain? Again, as a student of history, what do we hope to gain medium and long term by punishing Russia? Might not that have the effect—of poisoning the prospect for cooperation in areas in which we really need to be cooperating?

I wonder about just what the motive for sanctions is. Is it to change the regime? And if it is, maybe we ought to say so? You know—"we don't like you. We think you're doing a terrible thing—you know, we want to see you gone." And maybe they're—I don't know—maybe I'm being naïve as an academic, I don't know. But those were the questions I have to ask about sanctions.

Mr. PARKER. I have a number of people—I will recognize you—I've got it written down. I want to move Corrine, from the Embassy of Moldova, straight to the front of the list. Corrine, it's good to have you here today. Please.

QUESTIONER. Thank you so much, for organizing this event, Kyle, and thank you so much for the guest for this presentation. I would like to thank you as well, Matt, for mentioning Moldova, because it seems like it was a kind of, a little bit overshadowed by the events in Ukraine. I would like to stress that Moldova is as well one of the countries from the Eastern Partnership that expressed its interest to move closer to European Union, and that might be a little bit disturbing for someone. So my question would be, do you think that U.S. Congress is vocal enough with respect to Moldova at this point, and what would be your predictions or thoughts on the possibility of creating this corridor of protection between—that will interconnect Crimea, Transnistria, let's say another part of Eastern Europe, Eastern Ukraine, that some of analysts predicted before?

Mr. PARKER. Thank you, Corrine.

I'm going to take two quick questions, give the panel an opportunity to address. Don, I know you had a comment, and then I will close with a final question, move to bring this very interesting discussion to a close. Asta and then Karl.

QUESTIONER. I'm sorry I was late. All right. Well, I have two quick questions. One is, if we successfully apply the sanctions that we've—mechanism that we've learned on Iran to Russia, will it finally tell us if Russia is an oligarchy, which is what people have been arguing for the last—you know, after Yeltsin, or whether Putin has successfully mastered the bureaucracy, especially the police powers of the state—that he is now well on his way to dictatorship? So that's my first question about a, sort of, a hook on sanctions.

The second thing is, Matthew I want to thank you for finally saying something I could agree with you on.

You said, the West has been trying to integrate Russia into the modern world economic system for the last 20 years. You talked about a 21st century toolkit of sanctions, and yet your whole analysis of Putin ignores his 18th century, 19th century mindset of imperialism. He is one of the last imperialist leaders on the face of the globe. I mean, even the Chinese at least gave lip service to all of their ethnicities during their Olympics. All you saw during the Sochi Olympics were white, you know, white, blond, blue-eyed people. This is supposed to be a federation. Strobe Talbott has publically now said he doesn't believe Russia's a federation. There's no way it can be a federation. So it's the imperial mindset that makes his decision to ignore international law and international norms the problem. And I can't agree with you any, that we have a difference of opinion about what the problem with Putin is.

Mr. PARKER. Thank you, Asta. Karl Altau, from the Joint Baltic American National Committee. Karl.

QUESTIONER. Thank you, Kyle. Well, I agree totally with Asta, my colleague. Yesterday the Baltic—the Estonian, Latvian, and Lithuanian-American communities commemorated the 65th anniversary of the 1949 deportations. About 100,000 Balts were deported, by Moscow, to Siberia, and that's why we understand the nervousness of the Crimean Tatars. The Volga Germans were, you know, another group, and, I mean, Russia is, and the empire is, littered with all these people, so we're very nervous.

I mean, just a quick question: We've been kind of leading up to it, but how do all your calculations change when Russia—if Russia invades Eastern Ukraine next week, this week, or in three weeks?

Mr. PARKER. Thank you, Karl. Very quickly, Don, a comment, and then we're going to wrap this up.

Mr. JENSEN. OK. I want to make a comment. Karl, I agree with you. I hope there won't be. Tonya, your question was: Why don't we realize it's not the Soviet Union? I have an answer for that. One, then I would like a much more explicit repudiation of the Stalinist symbols, nostalgia and romance. It's still there on every May 1st, it's still there every day on TV, romance and—I would like a much more explicit repudiation of that. Point two: It's still an empire, whether it's Catherine the Great's empire, descended from—I've learned much more about that in the last few weeks. It's still an empire. That's why I think it's something to be objected to. A lot of countries are. You could argue the U.S. has a residual of it. But it's still an empire. And third: For me, one of the drivers of the current crisis is that a lot of the Kremlin elite, and I assume a lot of Russians, simply do not believe Ukraine is a separate country. And that drives a perception, it drives a commentary, it drives the propaganda. Putin himself said it.

I would like to see the Kremlin say that and act like it and not just this endless barrage of—they're not Russian speak—they're not they're not Russians in the Eastern Ukraine. They're ethnic Russian, Russian speakers, like—there're many multi-lingual societies. That would be my answer.

Mr. PARKER. Thank you, Don.

At this point I would like to—I hold one question in reserve, but I would like to offer the panel a minute each—very quickly, rapid fire—if you want to address the question from Karena (ph) on Moldova, from Asta on Iran sanctions and the imperial mindset, and from Karl on how does any invasion in Eastern Ukraine change any of what we're talking about today. Jim?

Mr. WARHOLA. One minute, right? Sure, yeah. OK. Yeah, back to the the Russian Federation, of course, you know, is not the Soviet Union, but there are enough echoes there to make more than a few of us here in the United States uncomfortable. I would, as you know, clearly agree. It seems to me, though, once again—to go back to some of my earlier remarks—that what seems to me is operating, is two fundamentally and probably irreconcilable differences about the nature of international order.

I think it's interesting that President Putin—or, excuse me, or, yeah, that President Putin again, constantly refers to Russia's national interests and so forth, and rightly so,

I suppose. President Obama refers to "the international community" again and again and again; not so much "the West" versus Russia, but "the international community." And it just seems to me that—we need to work towards some way to find some common ground to bridge those seemingly irreconcilable differences. And it won't be a matter of figuring out which one is right and which one is wrong, but attempting to look at things from the other side's point of view and begin to start building some bridges so that those two different conceptions—fundamentally, conceptually, theoretically distinct conceptions of world order—can begin to be bridged. If they don't, we're going to continue to be banging heads with Russia. And hopefully—there's going to be conflict, you know, conflict is a part of the human condition—but it doesn't have to take the form of violent conflict.

Mr. PARKER. Thank you, Jim. Matt: Moldova, Iran sanctions, East Ukraine.

Mr. ROJANSKY. Got it. Yeah, on Moldova, which was really a question about this Novaracia region being threatened, the answer is very simple, and that is that the reason Putin was able, with relatively little violence and at relatively low cost, to take Crimean territory from Ukraine was because a very large number of Crimeans were fine with that. And if you look at what people in Donetsk and Kharkiv and Odessa want and think right now, they are not the same as Crimea, but they are far from where they would need to be in order to make such a territorial grab unthinkable, both in terms of the unintended consequences if there were violence on the ground, and in terms of just objectively, you know—could a referendum, even pulled off under the appropriate conditions, give a result that is not the result you'd like to see? That is fundamentally about a vision for Ukraine that they like, that goes somewhere useful, and Ukraine's not there.

On Putin as an imperialist, I want to be very clear here: I don't care if he's an imperialist. The reason I don't care is, again, I don't particularly care about his psychology, except to the extent that it's useful in forging an American policy that advances our interests, and I don't believe it's in our interest to crusade around the world fighting imperialists. I think if we did that, A, it's an unbelievably dangerous slippery slope. I'm not sure what differentiates Putin's imperialism from Chinese imperialism, or Indian imperialism, or imperialism in any other continent on the world, and I don't think we want to get ourselves into that trap.

I think the challenge here comes from the fact that Putin is now both rhetorically and factually, in facts on the ground, challenging the status quo of borders after the collapse of the Soviet Union. He's saying that, with Russians being the biggest diaspora, the biggest ethnic—as you pointed out, Kathy ethnic, religious, whatever diaspora outside the borders of Rus in Europe, that these things now need to change, and that that's a grounds for changing them. We have legitimate objections, even if not to the idea of that, certainly to the process by which it was done, which is by force and a completely illegitimate referendum.

In order for us to have any credibility, though, in asserting those things, we have to undermine the arguments that Mr. Putin has been making. And that's why I go back to 2007, but frankly, long before that, and those are the arguments about our treatment of international law when it suits us and when it doesn't suit us; our use of force when it suits us and when it doesn't suit us. Again, the answer here lies not in being perfect angels and thus Putin will become a perfect angel himself. The answer lies in doing both walking and chewing gum at the same time, and that's why I talk about the weapons of the 21st century—the ones that we're going to use, because let's be honest, we're not going to send tanks in, whether it's Moldova, Transnistria, Odessa, Crimea—that's not what it's about. But we are going to use these economic weapons, so let's use them effectively at the same time that we defend our flank—and that is on our treatment of international law.

Mr. PARKER. I have a final question and then I want to bring this to a close. We like to start on time and end on time. We've been in a warm room and I appreciate everybody's attention and the good conversation.

My question is for both Jim and Matt—and Matt, you mention the OSCE, and I mentioned the Helsinki Final Act when we began—this is something, of course, very close to what we do here at the Commission on Security and Cooperation in Europe, the whole Helsinki process and commitments. With the—how did the Russian Foreign Ministry put it? I'm trying to wrap my mind around their phrasing. I think it's with the G–7's expulsion, or the G–7 left the G–8, right? So now that that's happened, one, it seems to me that that increases the relevance of the OSCE as a security forum to engage Russia, and I would just recall that we do this across three dimensions: the security dimension, the economic and cultural exchange contact dimension, and the human dimension. We at the Helsinki Commission focus on the human dimension, but we also address the other two dimensions. This is wrapped up in the OSCE's concept of comprehensive security—that these things are all related and interdependent.

I think of the Tsarnaev case that was recently in the news and us scratching our heads and wondering why we didn't have better cooperation, and couldn't we just have done something? At the same time I look at the rampant, ruthless, violent corruption in Russia's security services, and the reality that presents that we simply cannot cooperate in an effective manner with such a service. And so there you have something—rule of law, democracy—touching hard security, counterterrorism cooperation.

My question is—as you, Matt, had mentioned—that, you know, there's so little trust left in the U.N., the human rights commitment, the body of commitments we have in the OSCE is richer than the U.N.'s commitments in many areas, and I get the impression that Putin himself looks at this and views these commitments as essentially a product of Russian weakness in the 1990s. The question is, is there even less trust in the OSCE? And if that's the case, how viable a forum is this going to be going forward? Also, I would offer—I know I've been kind of a strict moderator the past 15 minutes, but any final comments, by all means, and then we'll send everybody on their way. Please, Jim, and then Matt.

Mr. WARHOLA. OK. My final comments—I mean, I appreciate very much the work that the commission is doing and the principles that undergird it, and I applaud their work. I honestly do, and I think it's good, and I think it's essential. an academic at heart. I'm not a policymaker, as you know. So I look at these things, I suppose, from an academic perspective, and what I've seen in the course of my life at the personal level, the national level, and certainly from the historical level, is that leading by example almost always gets one a lot more traction than words. The United States—we need to continue our own housecleaning and improving this republic as well. I don't think it ought to be done to the exclusion of taking on any kind of leadership role that the rest of the world would welcome.

I guess those would be my final comments, that the more we work on perfecting this republic—after all, women didn't have the legal right to vote in this republic until

131 years after it was established. We had a lot of work to do. We still have—and the list could go on and on and on. No one in this room needs to be reminded of the gap between the ideals and the reality in this country, and a lot of work needs to be done there. You know, to use a religious analogy, I suppose, if you'll indulge me for just a moment—Saint Francis of Assisi: some young convert to the Christian religion came to him; and he said, how, Saint Francis, how can I spread the good news of God's love all over the world? As Saint Francis said to him—he said: "Go and preach God's love everywhere you go—and if necessary, use words."

The example that the United States has presented, it seems to me, over the last 200 years is in a lot of ways more powerful than preaching. And how the world—or how that works itself out in terms of specific detail—that's the work that we need to do. But in terms of principle, that's the way I approach these things.

Mr. PARKER. Thank you, Jim. Matt—final comments.

Mr. ROJANSKY. Kyle, I just want to clarify—on the U.N., I was referring to Putin's view of the U.N. and international law in saying that there's not a lot of trust, not necessarily a general statement. He does not exclude the OSCE in the Munich speech. Here's what he says. I'm not going to read the whole thing. It's impossible not to mention the activities of the OSCE. As is well known, this organization was created to examine all— I shall emphasize this—all aspects of security: military, political, economic, humanitarian, and especially the relations between these spheres.

Could hardly ask for a better endorsement there, but then he talks about how it's being abused and manipulated along the same lines I described before. He says: We expect the OSCE be guided by its primary tasks and build relations with sovereign states based on respect, trust and transparency.

Here's the problem: It's the perfect versus the good. The OSCE gets us an awful lot of important stuff, but when poop hits the fan and things are really bad—like in Belarus in December of 2010—we're not going to be able to use the OSCE as a wedge to get in there and remove Lukashenko. What we are going to be able to get is some kind of mechanism to investigate, to find out what happened, to clarify, to bring attention to the issues, and maybe, gradually, over time, to build a consensus. That's what the OSCE gives us. Right now the OSCE has given us what? Some hundred or so observers on the ground who are going into Eastern Ukraine. No, they don't have a mandate to go to Crimea. The Russians vetoed that, if I understand correctly.

If we consistently ignore it because it is not, as I think Senator McCain has proposed, a union of democracies, sort of a union of the perfect which does only the good things and does them 100 percent, then we get nothing out of it, and that's a mistake, because we've got it today. And I think what the Soviet Union at that time did, and what the Russian Federation then accepted in accepting the Soviet Union's commitment under Helsinki, actually gets us a tremendous distance that we wouldn't if we tried from a tabula rasa today to do between the White House and the Kremlin. We wouldn't get that. And that's the vital importance of the OSCE. So it's the perfect versus the good.

Mr. PARKER. Thank you, Matt. I can only speak for our humble commission, but I can assure you we will not ignore it. We have not ignored it, and we will continue to put a focus on that through events like this, through our mission in Vienna, and in other ways.

I really would like to thank everybody for coming. I certainly want to thank our panel. Jim, it's so good that you came all the way from Maine to join us. Matt, it was fantastic to have you and to hear these different perspectives. Let me also recognize our fine interns, Caitlin Jamros, Simon Fuerstenberg, and Paul Massaro for their incredible work to put this together. As I mentioned, this is an on-the-record event. It will produce a transcript. We'll post it soon, and it'll eventually be printed as a formal publication of the Commission.

Check our website for future events. I hope this is the first of many conversations on Russia and Ukraine and the crisis. And with that, it is just about 2:45, and the meeting is adjourned.

○

This is an official publication of the
**Commission on Security and
Cooperation in Europe.**

This publication is intended to document
developments and trends in participating
States of the Organization for Security
and Cooperation in Europe (OSCE).

All Commission publications may be freely
reproduced, in any form, with appropriate
credit. The Commission encourages
the widest possible dissemination
of its publications.

http://www.csce.gov   @HelsinkiComm

The Commission's Web site provides
access to the latest press releases
and reports, as well as hearings and
briefings. Using the Commission's electronic
subscription service, readers are able
to receive press releases, articles,
and other materials by topic or countries
of particular interest.

Please subscribe today.